A Big
in c

THE SKINNY

ON

PARENTS

Mark Oestreicher

with Kami Gilmour

JESUS-
CENTERED

Guide your entire ministry
toward a passionate
Jesus-centered focus with
this series of innovative
resources. Harness the
power of these dynamic
tools that will help you draw
teenagers and leaders into a
closer orbit around Jesus.

The Skinny on Parents
© 2015 Mark Oestreicher

group.com
simplyyouthministry.com

Credits
Authors: Mark Oestreicher with Kami Gilmour
Executive Developer: Tim Gilmour
Executive Editor: Rick Lawrence
Chief Creative Officer: Joani Schultz
Editor: Rob Cunningham
Art Director and Cover Art: Veronica Preston
Cover Photography: Rodney Stewart
Production: Joyce Douglas
Project Manager: Stephanie Krajec

ISBN 978-1-4707-2087-2
10 9 8 7 6 5 4 3 2 1   21 20 19 18 17 16 15

Printed in the United States of America.

ACKNOWLEDGMENTS

Seems that, in a book about parents, I should start by thanking my parents: Dick and Bobbi Oestreicher. As a parent of a teenager and a young adult, I often reflect back to my own teenage experience, and my parents' rules and interactions. Three specific props I would give them for how they parented me as a teenager: They lived their faith actively, they were very fair with rules, and they were intentional about staying relationally engaged with me. Much of what I learned about parenting teenagers is merely a reflection of what I observed.

While I've had some parents in my many years of youth ministry that have been a royal pain, the vast majority of the thousands of parents I've interacted with have been amazingly supportive, helpful, and encouraging. I can't even start to list the best here, but I often (seriously—all the time) reflect on what some of those amazing parents would have done when trying to figure out how to parent my own children.

My wife is the best parent I know. The fact that we have a pretty good relationship with our kids and an above-average level of happiness in our home is dominantly a reflection of Jeannie's grace, insight, and commitment.

— **Mark Oestreicher**

THE SKINNY

ON

PARENTS

CONTENTS

THE SKINNY ON

PARENTS

BEFORE YOU GET STARTED

The book you're holding might be "skinny," but that's because it's all-muscle. This means that Mark Oestreicher and Kami Gilmour have cut away the fat and focused on the "first things" that make ministry to parents in youth ministry powerful and long-lasting. In our Skinny Books series, we've paired a thought leader (in this case, Mark Oestreicher) with a master practitioner (in this case, Kami Gilmour) as a one-two punch. We want you to be challenged and equipped in both your thinking and your doing.

And, as a bonus, we've added an Introduction written by Mark DeVries that explores parent-connections through the filter of a Jesus-centered approach to ministry. Jesus-centered is much more than a catchphrase to us—it's a passionate and transformative approach to life and ministry. Mark's Introduction to parent ministry first appeared in my book *Jesus-Centered Youth Ministry*, and we couldn't think of a better way to kick off this little book. It's time to get skinny...

—RICK LAWRENCE
Executive Editor of Group Magazine

THE SKINNY

 ON

PARENTS

INTRODUCTION

I taught my first parenting seminar at the wise old age of 20. Like a spring-loaded trap, I was happy to give this group of unsuspecting parents a piece of my mind, to let them know all the ways they were massively missing the mark with their children.

Today, I see things differently.

I'm a recovering parent of teenagers, and now I see how parents are the easy whipping boy of youth ministry. Too many youth workers (and youth ministry experts) rail against the failures of parents—failure to make their kids come to church, failure to keep their mouths shut when they feel like complaining, and failure to "support the youth ministry" (which often means an unwillingness to go on a weekend retreat when we ask them at the last minute).

As a youth worker who's also a parent, I've got no doubt which is the harder (and more important) job. When I do parenting seminars, I see desperation on so many faces— enough to know that parents of teenagers are exhausted. They're jumpy, anxious, nervous about the new, latest threat to their children's safety (and thus to their own parental sanity). The sad fact is that the blame game helps neither families nor youth ministries. We need each other.

This is a world that literally dis-integrates teenagers, forcing them into patchwork identities that grow out of disconnected relationships with adults who know nothing of each other. The centrifugal force pulling kids away from a convergent center in which they can develop an integrated identity is so powerful that it is perhaps only in a Jesus-centered faith community that young people in today's world can complete the identity-formation process. They need to hear their name, and therefore their identity, coming from the lips of Jesus. And that will only happen through a constellation of relationships with Christ-like adults for every teenager in our ministries.

One parent told me the experience of parenting teenagers feels like "being a dachshund in deep snow." I can relate. I've learned enough now to know that God never meant for us to do this parenting thing alone, especially parenting teenagers. Here's what binds us together: We both desperately need Jesus.

—Mark DeVries
President and Founder of Ministry Architects

CHAPTER

1

Trolls,
Death Eaters,
Parents,
and Other
Things We Fear

THE SKINNY ON

PARENTS

I was leading a mission trip in Mexico with a couple dozen junior highers. A few of the kids had spent one of our last days painting the exterior of the very small wooden house we'd built for a family. And two girls—Erin and Jennifer—had ended up, as painting teenagers are prone, completely covered in paint. I think they had as much paint on themselves as they got on the house.

Erin and Jennifer couldn't seem to get the dried paint off their arms. So, trying to be helpful (but not really knowing what I was doing), I drove to a small hardware store and bought some sort of turpentine or paint thinner. Honestly, I didn't completely know what it was, and my Spanish is very limited. But the girls used it to remove the paint from their arms, and everything seemed fine.

Until the middle of the night.

Erin and Jennifer came to my room and woke me up, crying, explaining through sniffs and overly dramatic groans that their arms itched like crazy. We ran their arms under water for hours. And once again, everything seemed fine.

Until we got home.

Jennifer's dad was livid. Rarely—in 33 years of youth ministry—have I had a parent unleash on me like that angry father did. He clearly knew more about Mexican paint thinner than I did (he was a scientist, and he schooled me in the difference between the chemical composition of our American paint thinners and what was likely the makeup of the substance in which his daughter had bathed her arms). He said I was irresponsible, and told me I should never be allowed to lead a group of teenagers. He told me that his daughter could have received a toxic level of something-or-other that could have led to something really bad or even death.

❯ A PARENT'S PERSPECTIVE *Kami Gilmour*

Safety counts—even in the details! Don't we all know to use latex/water-based paint? If paint isn't coming off skin, it's probably oil-based paint. And oil-based paint has harmful VOCs (really bad things to breathe in) that can cause respiratory distress and long-term damage to organs and central nervous system. Come to think of it, that paint probably had lead in it, too. The whole group was at risk with exposure to the paint—not just the turpentine girls! If I'd been a parent of a kid on this trip and caught wind of that father's anger, I'd be jumping on the panic bandwagon and researching the dangers, worried my future grandchildren would be born with a limb growing out of their forehead or something.

And this dad told me that his daughter—one of my leadership kids, who was a part of pretty much everything we did—would never participate in another trip that I was leading, ever.

I really didn't know how to respond. On one hand, he seemed right about the risk I hadn't been aware of. And on the other hand, I felt embarrassed (this diatribe took place in front of a large group of people). And I felt defensive, thinking, "Aren't you aware of everything I have *done* for your daughter?" I felt vindictive, thinking, "Do you even know what she *thinks of you*?" I was sure he was exaggerating. And hadn't he ever heard that you're supposed to sandwich criticism between praise?

My interaction with Jennifer's father rattled me deeply. And it touched on a reality that I find to be a common challenge for all youth workers (rookie or veteran, paid or volunteer): *Parents of teenagers are wild cards in youth ministry.* They can be your greatest ministry supporters and assets, or they can be your most significant impediments and challenges.

It always bugged me, as a young youth worker, when parents said or inferred that I didn't know what it was like to parent a teenager. But now that my own children are 20 and 16, I can look back and admit, "I didn't know what it was like to parent a teenager."

Sure, I had (and still have) plenty of insight: I'd
studied teenagers both in a theoretical sense and an
observational sense; I'd read more books about teenagers
than any parent I knew; I'd interacted with hundreds
(and eventually thousands) of real-life teenagers, many of
whom shared their deepest fears and hopes with me in a
way they might not with their parents; and I'd observed,
interacted with, and intervened with countless parents,
in good times and difficult times. I was an expert (as
are you, most likely) in adolescence. And I had a deeply
informed, mostly correct view of what makes great
parents and what makes less-than-great parents.

But I still didn't know what it was like to parent a
teenager until I had two of my own. So I'll likely
swap hats back and forth in this little book: parent of
teenagers, and veteran youth worker with a diploma from
the school of hard knocks.

Let's start with a goal in mind. In the olden days of youth
ministry, most youth ministry trainers and books would
tell us that we need to learn to work with parents. But
the subtle (and sometimes overt) message was: *We know
you are called to work with teenagers, but most teenagers
have parents, so you have to at least be aware of them.*
Maybe that's merely my revisionist memory, but the most
positive perspective I remember hearing in those days
was that we had to "understand teenagers as part of a
family system" to be effective. The message was: If you

don't know that a teen is from a messed-up home, you'll be limited in your impact.

But that mindset, and the approaches to ministry that we developed in those decades, is as riddled with holes as a zombie's sweater. Most (maybe all) of our practices of youth ministry had nothing to do with parents. At best, we tended to be intentional about communicating enough to keep ourselves out of trouble and oil the moving parts of our ministries (like, we communicated when we'd be home from camp, because we didn't like waiting around with that one teenager whose parents were always late).

I'm not trying to say that every youth worker was antagonistic to parents: Many of us just held the tainted and faulty working assumptions that our jobs and callings were limited to teenagers, and that parents were sort of beside the point. There was another ministry in the church for the adults.

But research and theological reflection and some honest dialogue (and the host of aging youth workers who are parents of teenagers themselves) are recalibrating our view of parents. Instead of asking didactic questions like "are parents good or bad?" we've been collectively putting on new lenses when we view parents.

⊙ A PARENT'S PERSPECTIVE *Kami Gilmour*

The majority of parents won't know what didactic *means, so maybe skip vocabulary like that in everyday conversation.*

Here's what I've observed as a fairly universal truth in youth ministry, with beautiful variety in how this truth is worked out in context:

Great youth ministries are passionate about helping parents—the key influence on teenage faith—succeed in their God-given roles.

With that goal in mind and that ministry lens in place, all youth workers—volunteer and paid, rookie and pro, childless or parents themselves—can and must be aware of a handful of realities. Some of these are perspectives to employ, while some are truths I've learned (more from parenting teenagers than from my practice of youth ministry).

PARENTS ARE NOT THE ENEMY

It's rare that I have ever heard a youth worker express these actual words: *Parents are the enemy*. But as I interact with youth workers, I find that our practices often reveal an underlying sense of this unspoken belief.

Of course, any youth worker who's been around the block a few laps can provide a real-life example of a time when a parent *really did* seem like the enemy—either because they treated us like an enemy or, more often, because we saw the destruction they were bringing to their teenager.

I think of the eighth-grade girl who was acting out sexually. And when I spoke with her single mom, I discovered that her mom was a prostitute (her exact words were, "I'm the classy type, not the sort you see on the street").

I think of the abusive father who occasionally hit his son, and constantly told him what a worthless piece of junk he was, how he would never amount to anything, and how the father wished the son had never been born.

Sadly, you might even have much more horrific stories of terrible parents.

But even while some parents, in some cases, might be extremely destructive to their teenage children, *most* parents aren't so easily classified or written off. You'll always find an exception (and you have to deal with the exception when you come across it), but the vast majority of parents truly desire good things for their children, even if they are confused about what those good things should be or how to help their children discover those good things.

With that conviction in mind, a great youth worker is forced to come up with a new way of perceiving parents. "Partners" works. So does "allies," even when parents aren't behaving like allies.

At the end of the day, if you want to be successful in helping teenagers grow in Christ, becoming healthy and whole people engaged in loving the world, then you simply *cannot* dismiss parents as enemies. Whatever your theory or theology, dismissing parents as enemies *does not* lead to the results we long to see in the lives of teenagers. It's counterproductive.

IGNORING PARENTS DIMINISHES IMPACT

So maybe you're thinking, "I *certainly* don't think of parents as enemies or treat them that way." But there's a scaled-back version I see in too many youth workers. And while we'd like to convince ourselves that we aren't anti-parent, we often deal with the uncertainty and the wild card by ignoring parents or gently keeping them at arm's length.

Plus, if you're a younger youth worker, the honest truth is that being around middle-aged parents can be massively awkward. I mean, if you're in your 20s, at least some of your teenagers' parents are the same age as your *own* parents!

Adding to the complexity of this is the fact that *you*, youth worker, can be awkward to be around also. Honestly, plenty of parents quietly think, "I'm very glad we have that youth worker at our church, and I'm sure he's wonderful, but I have no idea what to say to someone wearing a hat shaped like a giant salmon."

Even if you're a non-zany youth worker, you are, by assumption, intimidating. *You just might know stuff about me and our home that makes you think I'm a bad parent. So you make me nervous to be around.*

But this natural unease that *can* be present (it doesn't have to be, by the way) between youth workers and parents shouldn't be our excuse for avoidance. Just as I wrote in the previous section: Anything less than actively engaging parents, even when it's uncomfortable for you (or them), is counterproductive to the fruit you long to see from your ministry efforts.

Why? Parents are the biggest influence on the lives of teenagers. No way around that one. That's not always a positive influence, of course. (I know my influence on my own teenagers is a mixed bag.) But in terms of influence, research has shown us again and again that parents are numero uno. And you, youth worker, are likely somewhere further down the list (not even in the No. 2 slot), regardless of what teenagers might say.

If we want to see teenagers fully step into a life of faith, maybe we should obsess a tiny bit less about the influence of peers (which is usually No. 2 on the influence list), and a little bit more about resourcing, equipping, partnering with, and empowering parents. Makes sense, right?

MOST PARENTS ARE AFRAID

Let me start with myself as a case study here. Without being overly cocky, I think that I'm a pretty good parent.

I deeply know *about* teenagers, and I'm pretty sure I deeply know, at a personal level, the two in my home. I'm highly engaged, but not smothering. My wife and I are super-intentional about setting meaningful and helpful boundaries, increasing freedom, and following through on consequences. We love being with our kids, and all indications are that our kids love (mostly) being with us.

I'm not trying to say that I'm *The Best Parent You've Ever Met*, but I'd certainly squeak onto the honor roll, if even just barely.

Add to that: The youth ministry at my church is fantastic. We have all the stuff happening that I try to get youth ministries at other churches to embody. We have extremely talented and spiritual and personable youth pastors who know my kids and love them. And we have wonderful volunteers who lead well and enter into the real stuff of life with my kids.

But even with all that optimal stuff in place, I regularly freak out about my children. I have struggled to get to sleep, wondering if my son or daughter is going off the rails. I have reflected on some of their behavior choices and felt like an utter failure as a parent. And I have wondered if the next "inevitable" bad choice made by my own children will be the one that brings irreparable trauma, hurt, damage, or consequences.

I'm not a neuroscientist, but I do know that fear is a primal instinct that causes us to be reactionary. It comes from the part of the brain that initiates the "flight or fight" response, not the part of the brain where higher-level thinking occurs. In a state of stress or anxiety, the fear part of the brain triggers before the thinking part. This is important to remember when you think parents of teenagers are mentally impaired. We are afraid, not stupid (technically).

In short: I'm afraid. Not all the time, but I'm certainly afraid, as a parent, from time to time. And after interacting with thousands of parents, I can state with a high level of confidence that *most* parents of teenagers are afraid...

- that they're messing up their kid

- that they fall short as parents

- that their teenager will leave the reservation and depart from values and beliefs that the parent holds dear

- that their teenager is going to disengage from them and stop communicating (or that their teenager already has)

- that peers or culture are shaping their kid in ways they'll never be able to counteract

- that their kid will make that *one massive bad choice* that will result in colossal or even unthinkable consequences

I'm not suggesting that it's *healthy* for parents to operate from a place of fear. But I'm saying it's *normative*. And if youth workers can hold on to that likelihood when interacting with parents, it can reframe all sorts of interactions. Understanding that most parents are struggling with fear allows me, as a youth worker, to have compassion for parents, even when they're misbehaving.

◯ A PARENT'S PERSPECTIVE *Kami Gilmour*

Wow. I just read this section three times and it ministered to me. The fact that a longtime veteran youth worker/ teenage whisperer shares my parenting fears is reassuring. I always need to be reminded I'm not the only one.

Funny story: Years ago I attended one of Marko's youth ministry seminars on how to deal with parents. I knew Marko professionally before I took the seminar, but I had a guarded view of what this youth ministry expert would really say about parents. I braced myself for some bashing and mockery because my insecurities and fear as a parent naturally put me on the defense. But in the seminar, Marko shared his own fears and failures as a parent of teenagers with such transparency that I dropped my defenses and realized he was a true comrade. That was a defining moment for how I viewed Marko—he was an empathetic friend on this parenting journey. That's the kind of compassionate alliance parents are craving from youth workers! (And thanks for being real, Marko. Sorry I heaped extra guilt on you earlier about the Mexico incident—it was the fear talking! I'd forgotten that you really do understand this stuff and I can trust you to take care of my kids. I might even change my mind about sending them on a mission trip with you someday.)

MOST PARENTS WANT HELP

Picture yourself in a super-tough college class. This particular course isn't just difficult, it's also filled with lots of students who seem to understand the material in a way you never will. They regularly ask questions to which you don't know the answers—in fact, you don't even understand the questions. The professor seems to delight in these extra-sharp students, and that has you feeling very insecure. You *want* to do well in the course, and you're even somewhat interested in the topic, but you regularly feel like you're on the precipice of being exposed for the failure you're suspecting you are in this subject. And you're starting to fear that your final grade will reflect that failure.

Now, in the midst of class, you want to ask a question. But you feel like you *should* know the answer. And you are sure that others know the answer. Honestly, you're not even completely sure how to form the question! And if you *can* form the question, you have some sliver of concern that you'll look like an idiot, or be shamed. So you keep your hand down and don't ask for help.

That is not a crazy metaphor for how most parents of teenagers feel about asking for help. It might be a tiny exaggeration, but not by much. It's hard for parents to ask for help—but that does *not* mean that they don't want help.

If you, youth worker, can provide help in a way that allows them to not feel like loser, failure, idiot parents, then you will have both won them over and benefited the long-term vision of your youth ministry to teenagers!

❯ A PARENT'S PERSPECTIVE *Kami Gilmour*

Remember that helping parents doesn't mean you have to fix us or our kids. A great way I've heard this framed for ministry is "Be the shepherd, not the veterinarian." If a family's needs exceed your scope, help connect them to the right resources. What parents most often need are reassurance, perspective, and the knowledge that someone is willing to listen. It starts with an open invitation—make it known that you're available as an ally and guide. Your willingness to be there for us deepens the level of trust and loyalty we'll have for you.

THE SKINNY

ON

PARENTS

CHAPTER 2

*Four
Essential
Parent Ministry
Practices*

THE SKINNY ON PARENTS

If you're committed to actively engaging parents of teenagers and helping them succeed in their God-given role, then there are four essential practices that absolutely call for your intention and attention. Again, it doesn't matter if you're a rookie or veteran, if you're a volunteer, part-time, or full-time paid youth worker. It doesn't matter if you're male or female. And it doesn't matter if you're a parent yourself or not. *All* youth workers—of every stripe and variety—can and should be living into these four practices.

There *are*, however, three big variables that result in different manifestations of these four practices.

The first variable is *your time*. If you're a full-time youth worker—or even a volunteer youth worker with *lots* of time—your living out of these practices should be a major part of your week and even included in your job description. But if you're a volunteer with limited time, the way you live these out will need to be, by necessity, scaled back.

The second variable is *your context*. We can get ideas from each other and can even learn "best practices." But the best youth ministries are always contextual. For example, offering a parenting class or support group might be a perfect fit in some churches, and a complete failure or impossibility in other contexts.

The third variable is *you*. You are unique. You have experiences, abilities, knowledge, and insights that are exclusive to you. So how you live into these practices must flow out of who you are, not out of some sort of caricature of what you think (or someone else thinks) a youth worker *should* be doing.

The four practices are pretty straightforward: Listen, Communicate, Equip, and Invite. I thought about putting them in a cute little order that spells a word. But the only word I could come up with was LICE. And—ew—no one wants *that* as our mnemonic device for parent ministry. So let's just stick with Listen, Communicate, Equip, and Invite.

LISTEN TO PARENTS

You've probably heard someone say something like, "Showing up is 80 percent of life" (that's actually a Woody Allen quote). In a similar vein, I'd suggest that 80 percent of good parent ministry is listening. OK, maybe 80 percent is a tiny bit high—but let's call it 50 percent and we'll be about spot on.

Seriously, we ministry people—especially we *professional* ministry people—are so used to being the ones with the megaphones that it's easy to forget the massive ministry impact of listening.

The Gospels reveal how Jesus deeply listened to people—whether they were his followers or not.

And we don't merely listen in order to win the opportunity to unload truth (through correction or challenge or motivating pep talks). Andrew Root, in his bellwether youth ministry book *Revisiting Relational Youth Ministry*, challenges us that when we've talked about relational youth ministry, we've often been referring to nothing more than manipulation. We've *used* relationship as a *means* of getting certain results: compliance, decisions, attendance. Root makes the uncomfortable point that this is not how God comes to us in relationship.

In the same way, we can't use listening as a manipulative tool in ministry with parents. Listening is ministry in and of itself, not a means of getting somewhere else. And because parents are so often fearful of failure (or feeling like a failure) and are often nervous about asking for help, JOB ONE of great parent ministry is to listen, listen, listen. Other than the movement of the Holy Spirit, nothing will increase your ministry effectiveness with parents more than developing a reputation as a youth worker who's great at listening.

If you are younger, this is *even truer* for you. Honestly, you *should* have less to say—but you can soar to a nomination for *Best Youth Worker* simply by modeling, offering, and disciplining yourself for non-judgmental, grace-filled listening.

Schedule time for listening. Take parents out for coffee and focus on asking questions and listening (not sharing some agenda you might have). Make sure parent meetings have space when you're not the one talking. Host parent forums where you invite storytelling, sharing, and feedback. And constantly remind parents that you are available to listen.

By the way, we don't only listen with our ears. Listen with your eyes and your brain, too. In other words, *pay attention*, *notice*, and *observe*. Those are important listening skills for youth workers, whether you're in a literal conversation with a parent or not.

COMMUNICATE WITH PARENTS

If 50 percent of great parent ministry is listening, then the majority of the remaining portion is this second practice: Communicate. It might seem odd to include communication as a parent ministry essential. Even the shortsighted, dysfunctional youth worker who doesn't give a rip about parent ministry probably knows it's helpful to have some communication to parents.

But I'm not talking about marketing.

In a big company, the communication department and the marketing department aren't necessarily the same. That's because they fulfill different functions. I'm oversimplifying, and a business or marketing professor might object to my definitions, but marketing leads to sales, while communication leads to the recipient being informed.

There's no question that youth ministry requires a bit of marketing: You create that nifty PowerPoint image for your upcoming event because you want your group to consider coming to it. That's marketing.

But with communication, the "sale" isn't directly connected. Communication focuses on needed information.

I live in San Diego. But all my extended family and my in-laws live in the Detroit area. Pretty much every Christmas, my wife and kids and I travel to Michigan for the holidays. We try to use my airline miles for tickets, but this requires us to plan early and book our flights early, before the frequent-flier seats are gone. And every June or July, we start thinking about this trip. And every year, I realize that I don't have the information I need from my son's small private high school (where my daughter also attended, so this has been going on for years now) to plan the trip. Every year I have to send an email to the high school administrator asking if the dates for the school's Christmas break have been finalized. And every year I have to wait for a response before I can take action on planning our trip.

The school's *lack* of communication is an annual frustration. In this way, they are not "ministering effectively" to me as a parent.

The obvious parallel would be the youth worker who plans an important trip or event, but doesn't communicate the pertinent information (dates, times, cost, plans) until one or two months out. A teenager comes home from youth group and says how excited she is about a trip happening in six weeks, and can she "please, please, please" go? The parent realizes the trip is the same weekend the family has plans for a weekend in the mountains.

Now the parent is left with a lose-lose-lose set of choices: Cancel or move the family trip, or have the teenager skip the family trip, or tell the teenager she can't go on the youth group trip. Rather unintentionally, that youth worker has just lost trust with the parent.

Bad communication—or worse, a lack of communication—doesn't only result in inconvenience. Read this next line slowly and carefully: **The fastest way to alienate parents is to keep them uninformed.**

Of course, this isn't only about calendar stuff (though that's a major important place to start). Effective communication with parents is also about these things:

- Vision
- Purpose
- Values
- Boundaries
- Rules
- Teaching topics
- Problems and discipline
- Priorities
- Expectations
- Options
- And so much more!

A few additional communication realities also deserve naming...

You can't over-communicate. Repetition is fine, even good. It's very rare (mythical, even) that I've ever heard a parent say, "Our youth ministry keeps me *too* informed!" Sure, you need to learn to make communication clear and focused, providing the information that's really needed, on a timetable that's most helpful. But here's a good rule-of-thumb for knowing how much to communicate with parents: more.

Communication doesn't come naturally to a large percentage of youth workers. All sorts of personalities and skill sets can be fantastic youth workers. There's no reason to buy into the stereotype that a youth worker is always an up-front, energetic type who's fun and a force of nature. I've met some wonderfully amazing youth workers who are quiet, or more pastoral in their gift mix. And once in a while, I meet youth workers who are highly gifted in administration. But I think it's fair to say that *at least a large portion* of youth workers do not find administration and organization (of which communication is a subset) as their primary gifts.

For those of us who fit this description, we need to reframe the effort that goes into effective communication with parents. Instead of seeing it as drudgery or an annoyance, we need to reimagine communication as something that, when done well, frees us up to do more of what we really love to do.

A painter might not derive joy out of the task of preparing canvases. But if they really want to be in the zone and spend their time doing what they love the most and what they're gifted for and called to, preparing canvases sets them up for that. Same with good communication. Not communicating well will usually result in more time spent on stuff you're not stoked about (putting out fires, apologizing, answering email questions, losing trust).

Young youth workers often stumble in this area with parents. Again, I am not a fan of stereotypes, particularly stereotypes of youth workers (since I'm a youth worker). However, embracing the importance and practice of good communication with parents is all-too-often a lesson youth workers have to learn through missteps, failure, and negative consequences. Hey, I'm writing about myself here!

If you're a young youth worker, surround yourself with a few supportive, pro-you parents who can do a few things for you in this area:

- Ask them for guidance on what information is helpful to them, and on what timetable is best.

- Ask for input on what *means* of communication is most helpful to them. Do they want emails only? text messages? a Facebook page for parents? a blog with an RSS feed? smoke signals? all of the above?

- Ask them to hold you accountable to good communication, to let you know when they're feeling uninformed or when communication is late or incomplete.

- Ask them to give you a nudge *before* it's time for communication about a particular event or calendar item.

➲ A PARENT'S PERSPECTIVE *Kami Gilmour*

Great communication isn't just about giving detailed logistics in a timely manner. Some of the best communication I ever got was from a youth worker who sent an email to parents the day after our kids got home from a mission trip. He gave us a recap of the projects, the theme and Scripture of each day's devotions, and some simple conversation starters so parents could know how to ask relevant questions about the trip and initiate meaningful conversation. We were included and equipped in understanding what mattered most about that week through the follow-up communication. It was one of the most helpful emails I ever received.

EQUIP AND RESOURCE PARENTS

If listening is 50 percent of great parent ministry, and communication is another 30 percent, that only leaves us with 20 percent to spread over our final two parent ministry practices. Equipping and resourcing parents gets 15 percent, or three-fourths of that last bit.

Funny thing is, most youth workers think of this aspect of parent ministry first. Most youth workers think that if they want to engage in ministry to parents of teenagers, it necessarily implies starting parenting classes and launching parent support groups and creating a parenting lending library and a half-dozen other *programs*.

As a parent of teenagers, I don't need a youth worker to offer me a bunch of programs. I want your help, but I don't have time for a bunch of programs added to my life.

❯ A PARENT'S PERSPECTIVE *Kami Gilmour*
The people who show up for parenting programs usually aren't the ones who need it the most.

And as a veteran youth worker who has tried a wide plethora of parent ministry initiatives—some of which have been wonderful and others which have failed gloriously—I can tell you that adding a bunch of parent ministry programs is simply not where you should put your best effort.

Not that an occasional parent ministry program is a bad idea. Not at all. Just don't put all your eggs in that basket. And realize that it's likely that only a small percentage of parents will take advantage of a program you offer (especially if it requires time from them).

So, sure, planning an annual Parenting Summit or some sort of training dealio can be a wonderful thing. I speak for quite a few of these, and have seen them be a big win for youth workers who want to offer a one-time, focused training for parents. My own church hosts an annual parenting day on a Saturday, for parents of all ages. We start together and have an outside expert as a keynote speaker. Then we break up into "seminars" for some more specific training and conversation, based on the ages of our children. Since it has become an annual event, parents know to expect it, and our turnout has been fairly good. But we can't do that one very good parenting day and declare that we've fulfilled our need and desire to resource and equip parents.

Equipping parents needs to be part of our youth worker mindset, rather than a one-off program. And when you are constantly ruminating on how you can better resource and equip parents, you'll find myriad opportunities to do so.

Add bite-sized bits of training into an informational parent meeting. If you have parents in a room for any sort of information (such as a meeting to go over details about an upcoming mission trip), don't miss the opportunity to slip in some thoughts about what's going on in the faith development of teenagers, and why this trip fits in with those developmental realities. It only takes a few minutes to deliver some fantastic training content connected to the information the parents are present to receive, and they'll eagerly acquire more knowledge about their teenagers without realizing you were resourcing them.

Add equipping elements to written communication. Whether you have a parent newsletter or not, you certainly need to communicate regularly with parents. (See the previous section of this chapter!) This is *always* an opportunity to provide more than information.

Providing details on your upcoming small groups? Share a paragraph about how teenagers can verbalize their faith.

Reminding parents about summer camp registration? Add a few sentences about the role of milestones in the faith journey of a teenager.

Passing along details about a trip to a soup kitchen? Tell parents why "getting out of their comfort zone" is so critical for adolescents.

Remind them that they're the top influence in their teenagers' lives. Highlight an encouraging story about a parent in your group and the creative idea she had for her daughter's "rite of passage" ceremony. Share something you learned from the last youth ministry book you read. Pass along a key point you heard at a youth ministry training event.

Suggest books (or make them available). It's tough for parents to know what they should read, as there's so much unhelpful stuff out there. So make it a regular practice to suggest books that you think would benefit parents—even if you're not a big reader yourself! Just keep track of books that *other parents* mention as helpful, and pass along those recommendations. And if you have the budget (or can find a helpful donor), it can be a huge win to get bulk copies of a particularly helpful book, and give it away to all the parents (I've found that *short* books—which also happen to be less expensive—are the most likely to be read).

Pass along links to articles and blog posts. Honestly, many of your parents won't read a book you suggest or give them. But many more will read an online article. In emails you're already sending, add a link or two to online articles and blog posts that you'd recommend. Don't overwhelm parents with a dozen links—just give them one or two that you really hope they'll read.

Make connections. Just about the best help a parent can ever get is to hear from parents who've been through a similar situation to their own. Even if you're a 23-year-old rookie youth worker with zero parenting experience, you can still be an active networker of parents.

Send individual notes of encouragement. One of the most powerful ministries you can have with parents is when you pass along a word of encouragement about their teenagers. Remember, most parents have *at least some* fear when it comes to parenting. A short word of encouragement (either something great about their kid, or something you heard about or saw them doing) can be the high point of a parent's week. And it can have three additional benefits:

- Sending an encouraging note can open up communication for a parent to share more with you. Often when I send an email to a parent, that person then feels a sense of permission to respond with a question or a request for help.

- Sending an encouraging note can make it clear that you are in a parent's corner, which can be very important if and when you have to connect with him or her about something that's not as positive.

- Having a practice of regularly sending encouraging emails or social media messages to parents can have a positive impact on you, as your eyes will start to be more open to notice things worth encouraging.

❯ A PARENT'S PERSPECTIVE *Kami Gilmour*

I think encouragement is so essential that it should have more than a 15 percent importance weighting in the essential parent ministry practices. The ministry of encouragement is a big deal.

Parents are afraid, and encouragement is an antidote to fear. We don't hear that we're doing a good job. And we don't always get to see the positive things about our kids that you see. Help us believe we're doing something right and that we matter, because sometimes our kids don't seem to be responding. Remind us how amazing our kids are so that we can see them through that valuable lens.

I love the tips Marko outlined here—and I can't emphasize enough how welcomed and effective any of these things

*would be. Parents gravitate to what makes us feel
valued and what values our kids. With a ministry of
encouragement, you'll not only get parents' attention, you'll
also develop a deep appreciation and loyalty from us. And
most importantly, encouragement helps equip parents with
the confidence we need to be the kind of influencer you want
us to be in our teenagers' lives.*

INVITE PARENTAL INVOLVEMENT

Our final 5 percent of parent ministry is inviting parent
involvement. Limiting this to 5 percent doesn't mean it's
not important—it's just that it should receive less of your
time and attention than the other practices.

Frankly, you don't want every parent involved in the
youth ministry (that's obvious, right?). But young youth
workers often make the mistake of limiting volunteer
youth leaders to young adults.

Over and over again, I've seen parents of teenagers be
fantastic youth ministry volunteers. Sometimes middle-
aged parents of teens aren't as *available* as younger youth
workers, so you might not be able to expect the same
level of commitment or participation. But don't exclude
the possibility that they very well might be available.

The best teams of volunteer youth workers have diversity—diversity of gender and personality and race and socioeconomic status. And, maybe most of all, diversity in age. There's nothing quite as beautiful as a youth ministry team made up of a college student and middle-aged mom and a 30-something young married and a professional dad and a feisty old grandpa. Teenagers need all these different kinds of adults in their lives. So when we limit our teams to young adults, we're missing out on the wisdom and life experience that parents can often bring to the table.

I have a couple of rules for parents who might be involved in youth ministry as a volunteer: They can't be there to police the youth ministry or their own teenager, and it's best if they're not, whenever possible, their own teenager's leader (such as in a small group).

And if a parent doesn't have the time or inclination to lead a small group or play some other role on your volunteer team, you can still invite their involvement. Consider other support roles that parents can play, such as driving, providing meals, assisting with logistics for a trip, or helping coordinate communication with other parents (pro tip: start a parent prayer chain for the youth ministry, led by a parent).

In the middle school ministry that I'm a part of, one of my favorite volunteer leaders is a dad. He doesn't lead a small group (the role that most volunteers play in our youth ministry). Instead, he leads the middle school worship band. He doesn't *play* in the band. In fact, I don't think most of our middle schoolers who aren't in the band even know who he is. But he is faithfully there, providing leadership to the band rehearsals, helping select songs, coaching the band members on all aspect of musicianship and worship leadership, and being a part of a team. And I can say that I think his impact is substantially deeper on the kids in the band than my impact is on the guys in my small group, because he invests in them so deeply.

Stop to reflect on the three variables I mentioned at the beginning of this chapter that should shape your parent ministry approach.

The first of those was *time*. I'm a volunteer youth worker at my church, with roughly three to four hours per week to give to our youth ministry. Most of that time is taken up with preparation, actually leading my small group, and staying connected to my guys. So my parent ministry time is literally limited to roughly 15 minutes per week. I don't actually *do* something every week, so it's probably more accurate to say I give about an hour a month to parent ministry. But I'm still intentional about living into all four of these essential parent ministry practices. With my limited availability, these practices have to be "right-sized" so they don't overwhelm me.

The second variable was *context*. Your place of youth ministry is almost certainly different from mine. My context is a very casual, nondenominational church in a first-ring suburb of San Diego. It's a large but not massive church, with paid staff for our youth ministry. All of these uniquenesses factor into how I think about parent ministry, and even more so into how I practice parent ministry. Your context, and the parents in your church, should likewise have a big impact on your parent ministry plans.

The third variable was *you*. I'm a parent of teenagers, and that experience means I do parent ministry differently than I did when I was 25 or 35. I'm also a veteran youth worker with a good bit of knowledge about adolescence, so there are things I can offer that others might not be equipped to offer. But there are experiences and skills that you bring to your efforts of parent ministry that I would be sorely missing if I tried to bring what you can bring.

THE SKINNY ON

PARENTS

CHAPTER 3

*Exceptions
and
Extra Miles*

THE SKINNY ON

PARENTS

In addition to the four essentials of parent ministry, there are four other things that we need to think about when it comes to parents and youth ministry. Almost not intentionally, these four extra thoughts each happen to start with the letter C—making them a little easier to remember.

CRITICISM

It's simply impossible to avoid criticism in life. But serving in ministry to any age (children, adults, whoever) seems to result in a heightened quantity of criticism. Then, add a few more factors into the mix:

- Parents who are rightly and understandably protective of their children.

- Parents who are overly protective because today's culture tells parents they're abusive if they're not helicopter parents.

- Parents who are constantly wondering if their teenager is going to make a horrible decision that will redirect life in undesired ways.

- Parents who are regularly questioning their own approaches and are fearful that they're going to mess up their kid.

I think there's another factor to consider in this mix:

- *Parents who are dealing with some other major life pressure that make them feel out of control—such as divorce, job loss, financial stress, health scares, and other tough experiences.*

Stir all that together, and there's just no way around it: In youth ministry, you absolutely, positively, unquestionably will receive criticism from parents. Avoiding criticism is a fool's errand. Sure, we'd like to minimize criticism, and that's mostly done by exercising wisdom and communicating effectively. But even the wisest youth worker who communicates brilliantly with parents will be criticized. So the issue we need to wrestle with isn't avoiding criticism, but how to handle criticism when it comes.

Some guidance on how to handle criticism from parents:

1. *Read* Criticism Bites *by Brian Berry.* It's critical (ha!) reading for all youth workers. And especially if you're new to youth ministry, it contains needed and necessary wisdom in dosages that I'm not able to provide here.

2. *Remain open.* Discipline yourself to listen. Try to see past your defenses, past your good intentions that might not be acknowledged, and even past the tone and words used for the criticism. Try to put cloak yourself with an attitude of learning, that whatever the spirit of the criticism may be, there's probably something for you to learn. It might be criticism you *really* need to hear, something for which corrective action needs to be taken. But it's also possible that your learning from the criticism will have little to do with the actual complaint. Know that Jesus wants to use this criticism for your growth; he wants to use it for good.

3. *Ignore anonymous criticism.* This is tough to do and requires a fairly high level of discipline. You don't want to read that anonymous note, and you know it's going to hurt and make you angry, but you're somehow compelled. Resist that urge. Toss it. Ignore it. Pretend you never received it. If a criticizer isn't willing to speak to you, or at least put their name to the criticism, it doesn't deserve consideration.

4.   *Repeat back what you are hearing.* Listen to the criticism, and repeat it back in your own words, checking to see if you've understood correctly. Often, when parents level criticism, they have emotion or nervousness all wrapped up in it. When you repeat the criticism back in a distilled form (verbally, or in writing), without emotion, you provide an opportunity for clarity—and you'll often find that the parent will back down a bit and get more to the core of their concern on the second pass.

5.   *Commit to pray about the criticism.* Tell the parent that you're going to do this, and actually follow through. Ask God to help you see the truth and what issue you might need to address.

6.   *Look for the seed of truth.* I've often found that when I receive criticism from a parent, it's easy for me to focus on the 30 or 50 or 90 percent where the parent is wrong or misinformed. With prayer, I can focus on the 70 or 50 or 10 percent I'd be wise to address.

7.   *Use trusted parents for a second opinion.* It's wise and mature to run criticism from a parent past another parent—one you trust, and who has your best interest in mind—to get another set of eyes on the issue. This will help you sort out what needs to be addressed and changed, from what merely needs a gracious response.

8. *If the criticism is over something serious, loop your supervisor into the conversation.* This might sound like a risk (and it can be, depending on your supervisor). But if the criticism is a big deal, you're at greater risk if you keep it to yourself.

9. *Try to get back to the parent and close the loop.* If you don't respond, or if you put off responding for a long time, a small criticism that could have been easily resolved may blossom into a massive problem with long-lasting consequences and tension.

⊙ A PARENT'S PERSPECTIVE *Kami Gilmour*

I don't call our youth pastor every time I think about the ways he's championed my son's walk with Jesus. I usually forget to thank him unless the occasion arises, even though I'm silently grateful and aware of his influence on my son's life every single day. But I don't hesitate to pick up the phone when I'm upset that he crammed 12 kids in his SUV for a lunch outing, or when he shot my son execution-style during paintball.

So keep it all in perspective. Unhappy people are much more vocal than happy people. For every criticism, there are 10 unspoken "thanks" you'll probably never hear. Don't let a critical comment become the defining voice of the value of your ministry.

CHANGING YOUR PARENT MINISTRY GOGGLES

If you stick around in youth ministry for a while, you'll discover that you have to make some changes in how you approach things. You'll likely engage in the *practice* of youth ministry differently at 40 than you did at 23.

And your relationship with teenagers will (and should) change, too. I found, in hindsight, that I related to teenagers sort of as an older brother when I was in my 20s. Then, in my 30s, I started sensing that I was more like an uncle. Somewhere in my 40s, I discovered that some of my students' parents were the same age as me, and suddenly I realized that teenagers were starting to relate to me as a parent figure (in a good way).

In the same way, you'll discover that your ministry with parents also will shift over time. Some of this comes with longevity—staying in one church for a number of years allows you to build trust and credibility with parents. But even more so, as you move into different life stages yourself, you'll discover that parents interact with you differently.

This might seem unfair, but it's completely natural. When I'm interacting with a random person about being a parent, my conversation with them is very different if they don't have kids of their own.

My wife and I married fairly young (21 and 22). But we waited a bunch of years to have children. So I was 30 when had our first child. And I instantly noticed two things in my interactions with parents: First, they viewed me through different lenses, now that they knew I also was a parent; and second, I discovered that I viewed parents through different lenses, too, since I now understood what it *felt like* to be a parent.

Athletes wear different-colored lenses to help them in varying light conditions. This has been a helpful metaphor for me. I think of my life stage as a set of goggles with colored lenses. As I move into a new stage of life (particularly one that involves parenting), I swap out my parent ministry goggles for a new set. And this allows me to intentionally engage parents on a different level.

Canadian youth ministry expert Marv Penner wrote a great book years ago on parent ministry (*The Youth Worker's Guide to Parent Ministry* is still in print—it was published in 2003, so it might feel dated at points but remains a very helpful book). In it, Marv lays out a pyramid of parent ministry practices, with increasing levels of intensity. In order from least intense to most, the nine levels are:

- Acknowledge

- Affirm

- Communicate

- Encourage

- Connect

- Equip

- Involve

- Educate

- Co-Nurture

In some ways these are an expanded version of the four essential practices of parent ministry I laid out in Chapter 2 of this book. But where I found Marv's book particularly helpful was in his suggestion that we youth workers *mature* into our ability to effectively operate at these different levels of parent ministry as we grow older and move through our own life stages.

For example, parent ministry is a very different animal for me today, as I'm able to relate to parents as a true peer. In some cases, I even relate to parents as someone who's a life-stage ahead of them, as someone with *more* parenting experience (particularly when their kids are just coming into the teenage years).

But this isn't only about *how* you do parent ministry or *what*, specifically, you offer parents. It's also about your goggles—your perspective. When I'm interacting with parents of teenagers these days, I'm more often reflecting and encouraging and challenging based on my experience of parenting teenagers (my current goggles) than from my perspective as someone who spends time with teenagers (my former goggles).

In the coaching work I do with youth workers, I often find that the biggest mark of a mature leader is the youth worker's self-awareness. **Your self-awareness about the perspective you bring to parenting, which filters into every interaction with parents and every attempt at parent ministry, is a critical component of your effectiveness.**

Don't apologize for your life stage; own it. But be aware of the strengths *and* limitations your life stage brings— the goggles you're wearing—to your parent ministry.

CYB

I opened this little book by stating that parents are a *wild card* when it comes to youth ministry. They can be your best assets and supporters, or your most troubling speed bumps and challenges.

The largest portion of whether parents are *for* you or *against* you is in your control. If you are relentless and intentional about living out the Four Essential Practices of Parent Ministry in a contextualized way, you'll win over the vast majority of parents.

But no matter what you do, you'll still have the occasional parent who seems devoted to reeking destruction, who wants to hurt you, or who's convinced that you are irresponsible or misguided. In these cases, it's critical that you are savvy enough to Cover Your Behind.

Two case studies from my own experience might be instructive here:

In one church I had a Youth Ministry Council (an official body with authority over the ministry but not over me) made up mostly of parents. I was a rookie youth worker who occasionally made bad choices, as is common for rookies. My intentions were good; I just didn't have the wisdom or experience to consistently make decisions that parents would be comfortable with.

I think this council *wanted* to support me. But each time we discussed a decision I'd made that was less-than-wise, I was defensive and manipulative, and I used redirection and partial information to keep their attention off the real issues. As a result, this group turned against me. This shift happened gradually, but I wasn't wise enough to see it happening. And when a particularly critical issue arose where some accusations were being made against me, the Youth Ministry Council didn't support me, and I found myself exposed and vulnerable (in a way that ultimately led to being asked to leave).

At another church, years later, I instituted a Parent Advisory Team. This group didn't have official authority, but I empowered them to make decisions and give input. On a particular winter retreat, we'd partnered with another church. The other youth pastor wanted to do a crowdbreaker that I found too risqué and crude. I pushed back, but he was insistent. So I relented, with the condition that he wouldn't involve students from my youth group.

But in the end, I *knew* it was inappropriate—and I knew parents from my church would hear about it. So upon our return, I called a meeting of the Parent Advisory Team. I shared the whole story with them, not defending myself (admitting that I should have drawn the line more firmly). I asked for their forgiveness, and I asked if they would support me if and when other parents complained. They totally had my back, because I'd empowered them and had proven trustworthy (even though I'd made a bad choice). They asked that if any parents contacted me I would direct the parents to them, and they explained to the complaining parents that we had talked it through and that I had their unreserved support.

As you can see from these two stories, the core issue here is honesty. But there are two more important practices when it comes to CYB:

- *Document the situation.* When a parent starts causing problems, confronts you over an issue, or sends a complaint email, keep a digital record (or what used to be called a "paper trail"). Summarize the issue, the complaint, and your response. Make sure it's dated. If new issues or subsequent interactions occur, add them to the same document. This digital record can seriously help if the issue ever becomes a full-blown witch hunt or trial (I don't just mean an actual legal trial—many youth workers are "put on trial" by their pastors or church boards).

- *Don't let your supervisor get blindsided.* Even though it might be uncomfortable and awkward, you are exercising wisdom when you loop your boss in on any confrontation with a parent. Most times you won't need their help (and you should clarify that—ask for help when you need it, and be clear that you're not asking for help when you don't need it). But keeping confrontations with parents private is *not* in your best interest. The last thing you want is your senior pastor coming to you, after speaking with an angry parent, asking you, "Why didn't you tell me about this earlier?"

These elements of CYB are essential to mature leadership.
It stinks to have that parent out for your throat, but
maintaining integrity throughout the process is essential.
I'd add another "D" to the list: "Direct communication."
As Marko said, be on the proactive end of documenting
and communicating with those who need to be in the know.
But avoid the trap of venting to people who aren't directly
involved. You might have a good relationship with another
parent and want to share your frustration about the
difficult parent, but don't be the person who bad-mouths
a parent to another parent. It can backfire. Stay above the
line and embrace the posture of a mature leader. Focus on
maintaining good relationships with other parents without
bringing the drama into it. You'll be perceived as more
trustworthy in the long run.

CURIOSITY

This last C is a principle I learned years ago from a
consultant who was working with a leadership team
I was on. Our team appeared to get along well on the
surface, but there was underlying competitiveness and
conflict. We experienced a major shift in the way we
worked with each other when we learned to be *curious*
about each other's intentions.

Curiosity might have killed the cat, but it's a massively helpful practice in human interactions, particularly when there's tension or conflict. I've since found this to be true in all human interactions—looking for the other person's "positive intent" changes everything. Ask yourself, "What is it that they're hoping to achieve?" and "What might be behind this presenting issue?"

This is so true in parent ministry. If you can learn to exercise curiosity in your interactions with parents— whether those are upbeat and positive interactions or challenging and confrontational interactions—you can gain a few things:

First, exercising curiosity removes your defensiveness and puts you in a position to be gracious, patient, and sympathetic (characteristics that reflect the heart of God with us, by the way).

Second, exercising curiosity de-escalates an otherwise tense interchange. When your perspective is focused on "How can I help you get what you want?" rather than "How can I defend myself or get what I want?" you disarm your confronter (usually). Your perspective and vibe allow the parent to relax and not be so convinced that they're going to have to fight for what they want, even if they aren't completely sure what they want.

Finally, exercising curiosity allows a pathway to get at the real issue. And this can lead to a positive outcome for both the parent and you. Repeat back what you think you're hearing and ask if you've understood correctly. Then ask questions like, "Are there other issues that are a part of this?" and "Could you help me understand the result you'd like to see?"

❯ A PARENT'S PERSPECTIVE *Kami Gilmour*

I love this posture of curiosity. And this also points back to the practice of listening with the intent to learn. Being a curious listener is a great combo!

THE SKINNY

ON

PARENTS

CHAPTER

4

*Thanks,
From a Dad
of Teenagers*

THE SKINNY PARENTS

Yes, I'm a youth worker. Been at it for a long time now.

But I have a more important identity and role when it comes to teenagers: dad.

One of my kids is basically done with her teenage years. She's 21 and a sophomore in college. The other one is solidly a teenager: my 17-year-old son, who's a junior in high school. I like lots of teenagers, but I'm pretty preferential to my own. They are not perfect, but they are awesome. They are flawed, but they are breathtaking. They can be annoying, but they are the greatest joy of my life.

As I wrap up this short book, I'm writing to you, youth worker, while wearing my dad hat. And while this could be read to the literal youth workers at my church (and would be accurate), I'm thinking about all of you when I'm writing this.

Let me start with this: *Thank you*. Really. Those two little words hardly say it. I know the toll this takes on you, I know the cost, I know the stress, I know the hours. I understand what you give up, because you *can't not* do this—the calling in your gut compels you. I don't only know this because I'm a youth worker—I also see this as a dad. I see you giving up time. I see you sacrificing. I see you putting up with stupid red tape and politics and agendas from the church and from other parents and from the students and—if I'm honest—from me.

I know I didn't read your email with the details, and as a result...

- We didn't turn our deposit in on time (and you were gracious about that)

- We asked questions you'd already answered (and you were gracious about that)

- I texted you asking when it started, or when the cars were leaving, or when they were returning (and you graciously responded)

That time I was freaking out about a choice one of my kids made, you calmly assured me it would be OK and that my kids were lucky to have me as a dad. I needed to hear that, way more than you could possibly realize.

That time you said that encouraging word to my kid had an impact far greater and longer and wider than you would have imagined. Not only did you help my kid, you encouraged me (deeply).

Don't be overwhelmed, my friend. We parents (well, at least most of us) don't want to take all your time. We don't want to change you. We are immensely grateful for how you bless us and our kid with your time and focus.

Just remember that we're here, please. Remember that we care passionately about our children and would sacrifice our own lives for them if necessary. Remember that we mean well, even though we're not perfect. Remember that we're afraid we're not doing this well and our precious children are going to go off the deep end because of our inadequacies.

We don't need you to reinvent your entire ministry to come hold our hands. But we need you to communicate with us. We need you to listen. We need you to be curious about our motives and assume good. We'd love you to tell us what you're seeing about teenagers and youth culture and—especially—our own son or daughter.

If you do those things, we will be so blessed and grateful, that we will forever be your biggest fans. We will speak highly of you and praise you to all peoples!

With all the buzz these days about parents (and dads, specifically) taking back the responsibility of the spiritual nurture of their kids, I want to go on record as strongly as I am capable of stating this, straight from my heart, with everything I know and believe:

While I do take responsibility for my kids, I need you. My kids need you. **Please, please, please never buy the lie that you aren't needed. Please don't question your calling. Please don't fall prey to the "let's do away with youth ministry" crazies.** I need you. My kids need you. My wife and I cannot be the only spiritual voice in their lives—God never intended that to be the case!

I know that you actually like my kids. Do you have any idea how much that means to me as a parent? You choose to be present to them. You choose to challenge them and encourage them and laugh with them and pray with them. That, my friend, is irreplaceable.

Thank you.

Thank you.

Thank you.

And may God richly bless you, as you have blessed me.

❯ A PARENT'S PERSPECTIVE *Kami Gilmour*

Amen! Ditto times a million. Thank you, youth workers— from a mom who's grateful beyond words, and for the many thanks that have been left unsaid. Thank you for supporting me as a parent and making this less scary. Thank you for loving my kids. And thank you for loving Jesus enough to put up with all of us.